BRITAIN IN OLD P

KINGSTON, SURBITON AND MALDEN

TIM EVERSON

BUDDING BOOKS

A Budding Book

First published in 1995 by
Sutton Publishing Limited
Phoenix Mill · Thrupp · Stroud
Gloucestershire · GL5 2BU

This edition first published in 2000 by
Budding Books, an imprint of Sutton Publishing

Reprinted in 2001, 2006

Title page: Cottages in Union Street, 1897.

British Library Cataloguing in Publication Data.
A catalogue record for this book is available from the British Library.

ISBN 1-84015-176-5

Typeset in 9/10 Sabon.
Typesetting and origination by
Sutton Publishing Limited.
Printed and bound in the USA.

To my wife Shaan, who is the prettiest picture I know

Kingston Market Place, 1911. Kingston's market was a livestock market until 1925 when a sheep upset customers by wandering around Boots the chemists. The livestock were then transferred to the Fairfield.

Contents

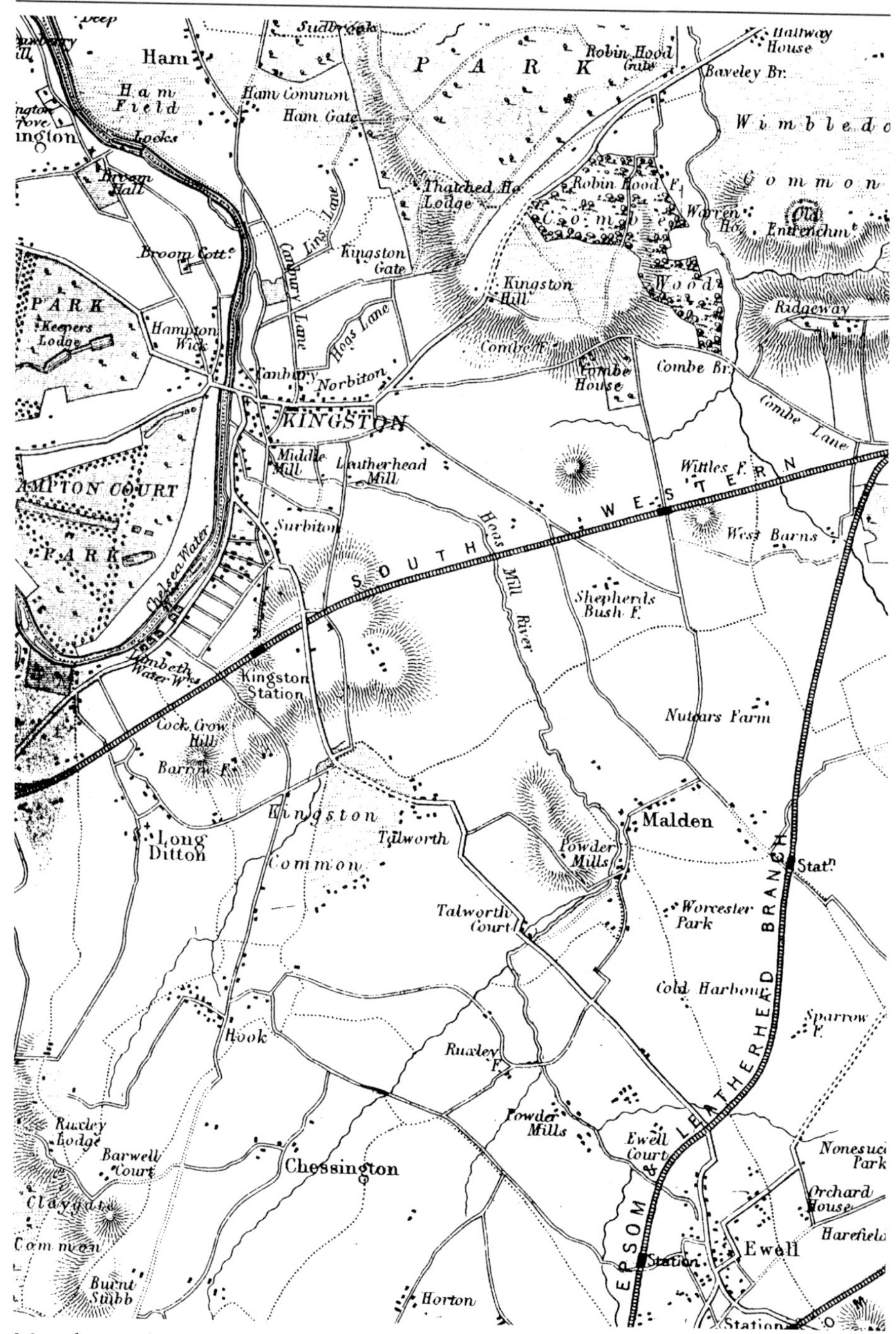

Map from *The Dispatch Atlas* of 1863 showing the district just before the railway reached Kingston.

Introduction

Although dominated by Kingston town, this book endeavours to cover all the area now encompassed by the Royal Borough of Kingston upon Thames. I have tried to find reasonable photographic coverage for the smaller villages like Hook and Coombe, and more recent suburbs like Tolworth, as well as Surbiton and Malden, which were large enough to have their own local government from the mid-Victorian period, although since 1965 they have been amalgamated with Kingston.

Kingston is first mentioned in a charter of 838 when a council was held there by King Ecgbehrt, and in the tenth century it was the coronation place of seven Saxon kings of England. In Domesday Book it is mentioned as having five mills, probably water mills, on the Hogsmill river and three fisheries, from which it later took its coat of arms – three salmon on a blue background. Kingston was granted its first charter in 1200 by King John, and a long series of royal charters followed which gradually extended the rights of the people of the town. Edward IV incorporated the borough in 1481 and Charles I stated that no other town within seven miles was to hold a market, a right still in force today. Because of this right and because of its position as a crossing point on the Thames, Kingston has always been a major shopping centre attracting traders and customers alike from a wide area.

Like many other towns, the biggest change in Kingston's life was the coming of the railway in 1863. This added greatly to the population and caused a housing boom which meant that much of Kingston's open land was developed by the 1890s when many of the photographs in this book were taken. Kingston was an agricultural and market town until the nineteenth century when several industries developed. On the riverside there was a tannery, a timber yard and, of course, boat-building. When a decline in agriculture resulted in a reduction in the amount of grain that needed to be ground into flour, the water mills turned to other work, such as the grinding of linseed for oil or coconuts for fibre matting. Brewing was very big business in Kingston and, from 1912, so was aircraft production. The market began by selling mainly livestock and farm produce, but grew into the general market which is still with us today and which now competes with the shopping centres. Much of the heavy industry has gone.

Norbiton is first mentioned in the medieval period along with Surbiton. The names mean north and south granges or granaries, and they were the agricultural stores for Kingston. The part of Norbiton nearest Kingston along London Road was soon built up in a long ribbon development, and by 1841 the population was large enough to form its own parish. It is still mainly a residential area today.

Surbiton was purely farmland until the early nineteenth century when some large houses were built there. One of these was Southborough House, built in 1808 by John Nash. Development was slow, however, until the coming of the railway in 1838. Due to problems with landowners and opposition from the coaching trade, the people of Kingston rejected the railway when it was offered to them in the 1830s – a rejection they later bitterly regretted – and so the first railway in the area went through Surbiton on its way from London to

Portsmouth. People immediately flocked to the area in order to commute to London, so the housing boom in Surbiton predated Kingston's by twenty-five years. Surbiton was still governed from Kingston's town hall, but the district's development made its inhabitants strive for their independence, which they achieved in the form of a board of improvement commissioners in 1855. This board became an urban district council in 1894 and a borough in 1936, before being reunited with Kingston in 1965. Since both Kingston and Surbiton front on to the river, and so many of the river scenes included in this book could be classified as either Kingston or Surbiton, all the river scenes have been collected together in one section.

Tolworth is first mentioned in Domesday Book, but the manor here consisted of little more than a couple of farms until the 1920s when, helped by the new Kingston bypass, it became a vast suburban housing area before the Second World War.

Hook likewise was only a small village for much of its past, growing in size with the building of the bypass and forming the southern limit of London's urban spread. Chessington is also mentioned in Domesday and is the only part of Kingston borough that is 'rural', although it has not entirely avoided surburban growth. It is famous these days for its zoo and theme park.

Coombe can also trace its history back to Domesday when it was a small hamlet. In the nineteenth century the Manor of Coombe was owned by the dukes of Cambridge who built up a large estate. From the 1860s this began to be broken up for housing for the gentry, and notables such as John Galsworthy and Lillie Langtry lived there. Both Coombe and Kingston Hill (also part of the Duke of Cambridge's estate) are still sought-after residential areas today.

Old Malden is another Domesday village. Its name means 'cross on a hill'. It was given the name 'Old' in the 1870s to distinguish it from New Malden. The latter is further to the north and sprang up as a result of the building of Malden railway station in 1846. The land here was originally part of Norbiton Common. Like Surbiton, New Malden became disenchanted with rule from Kingston and gained its own local board in 1866. It incorporated Coombe and Old Malden and became an urban district in 1895. Again like Surbiton, Malden & Coombe became a borough in 1936 and was absorbed back into Kingston in 1965. It too has its own shopping high street and other facilities, but is mainly residential. New Malden also had a housing boom in the 1920s and '30s which filled all the open space to Kingston, Surbiton and Tolworth in the west, and Motspur Park and Worcester Park in the east.

Such is the brief history that makes up the many facets of this London borough. Closely connected throughout their history, these districts probably make up one of the closest-knit of the London boroughs, with boundaries stretching back into the distant past rather than recently invented. Through this selection of photographs, it is hoped that the reader will see something of this past from the separate communities of the Victorian period through to the surburban growth of the 1930s. Some later photographs are also included to show that places are still changing. Remember, the snap of today is tomorrow's historical photograph.

Section One

KINGSTON

Five views of Kingston from a postcard used in October 1959, showing river views that can still be seen. The Market Place and Clarence Street have both now been pedestrianized. Kingston Bridge is due to be extensively repaired in the late 1990s.

An empty Kingston Market Place photographed by Walter Hodgson of Kingston Photographic Society in 1897. The Market House was built as a town hall in 1840, replacing an earlier building. Above the door is a statue of Queen Anne taken from the former town hall.

Kingston market day (Saturday), 1898. Saturday was general market day as opposed to livestock market day which was Thursday. Produce predominates as it does in today's market.

The Shrubsole Memorial fountain photographed by G.T. Jones in 1895. Henry Shrubsole was a popular banker who was three times mayor of Kingston, dying in office in 1879. This memorial was paid for by public subscription and was unveiled in 1882.

The town hall (now called the Market House) decorated for the coronation of Edward VII in 1902 and photographed by Walter Hodgson.

The Market Place from further south, May 1900. The photograph was taken on a Saturday and it shows a horse bus crowded with market-goers. The decorations are to celebrate the relief of Mafeking.

The north-west corner of the Market Place, 1897. The Olde Segar Shoppe is now part of Next and is one of Kingston's oldest buildings dating to *c.* 1500. Thames Street is in the background with Rabbits, the bootmakers, and Mangers, the drapers, on the left.

The demolition of the Sun Hotel, March 1931. One of Kingston's best loved old coaching inns (along with The Griffin), the Sun was famous for its riverside gardens.

Healey, pork butchers, in the Market Place, *c.* 1903. There had been a butcher's shop here since at least the seventeenth century; the last one closed in 1973. Down the right-hand side is Harrow Passage, leading to the Apple Market.

The Jacobean staircase from the Castle Inn, 1898. This old Kingston inn had become part of Kingston's earliest department store, Clarkson, in the early eighteenth century. After various renamings, this store closed in 1987. The staircase is mentioned in Jerome K. Jerome's *Three Men in a Boat*.

The back lane by the side of the Sun (on the left), leading down to the river where pleasure steamers could be boarded for Oxford.

Another back lane, photographed like the previous one in 1897 by Walter Hodgson. This one is King's Passage off Thames Street, also leading (eventually) to the Thames.

Harrow Passage, looking from the Apple Market through to the Market Place, 1897. The Old Harrow on the left was another old Kingston public house which became a shop in 1925 and is now a baker's.

The Apple Market with the Old Harrow and Harrow Passage on the left, 1903. In the distance it narrows into Crown Passage before joining Church Street.

The Apple Market from Eden Street, 1959. There are still market stalls here today, but the lovely little tiled roofs were taken down in the 1970s.

The Coronation Stone on which seven Anglo-Saxon kings were allegedly crowned. It is sitting on a plinth and surrounded by railings dating to 1850, when it was set up to the south of the Market Place. This photograph is from 1904.

The Coronation Stone and railings, 1955. The stone is in its current position in front of the Guildhall near Clattern Bridge. It was moved here in 1935 following the building of the Guildhall.

A Thomas Tilling horse bus plying the Kingston–Richmond route, *c.* 1912. The bus is in the Market Place standing in front of The Druid's Head inn.

Trams arrived in Kingston in 1906 and were immensely popular. Here is a No. 233 en route to Kingston. Neither the exact date nor location are known.

In 1931 London United Tramways replaced its trams with trolley buses, which were known to the public as 'silent death'. This trolley bus is pictured with its proud crew in 1932.

One of the earliest known photographs of Kingston, showing All Saints Church from the Market Place. It was taken by a Mr Kenrick in 1866.

All Saints Church from Church Street, *c.* 1900. Originally a Saxon foundation, the present Norman church was heavily rebuilt in the eighteenth and nineteenth centuries, and the tower was refurbished in the twentieth century.

J. Butler Pinx. Jas. Mc. Ardell Fecit.

Estr. Hammerton

Late Sexton of Kingston upon Thames

N.B. She was miraculously preserv'd under the Ruins of the Church, which fell down as She was digging a Grave there, in the Year 1731. And notwithstanding She lay cover'd 7 Hours yet She surviv'd the Misfortune 15 Years.

Esther Hammerton was born 1711, died 1746. At the accident above related her father, who was sexton, and two other people were killed, and she received a hurt which prevented her from ever wearing stays. In consequence of this and of her occupation in her father's position, she ever afterwards used men's garments.

Hester Hammerton is one of the more famous Old Kingstonians. The author has recently discovered that he is related to Hester.

All Saints Church from Clarence Street, *c.* 1905. The graveyard was full by the 1830s and people are now buried at Bonner Hill Road. The gravestones have been moved to the sides and this area has been landscaped.

Kingston Baptist Chapel in Union Street, 1902. Built in 1864, it stands next to an old nightwatchman's shelter which was at this time serving as the town mortuary.

The 1953 Remembrance Day Service in the memorial gardens near the old mortuary, which is next to the church. The mortuary has now been turned into a two-storey pseudo-medieval building and has become a fancy baker's.

Thames Street from Clarence Street. The over-the-top decorations are to celebrate Queen Victoria's Diamond Jubilee in 1897. Notice the futile attempts to stop the man in the middle of the picture from moving!

Slums in Kingston, 1895. This is Water Lane a few years before the slums were cleared. It is now covered by Bentall's car park. This photograph is by George Ayliffe whose reminiscences were published by the *Surrey Comet* in 1914.

Old Bridge Street, which used to lead to the wooden bridge across the Thames, serving Kingston until 1828. The Black Lion public house is on the right with Gridley Miskin's timber yard in the distance. This photograph was taken at 2.15 p.m., 26 August 1896.

The Row Barge Inn in Old Bridge Street, 1906. Dating from the seventeenth century, the inn was virtually rebuilt in 1900. It was demolished to make way for the John Lewis development in 1986.

Fountain Court, Thames Street, February 1898. This little courtyard and well were demolished in 1937. The site is now (1995) occupied by Halfords.

The Rose and Crown in Old Bridge Street, 1896. A medieval undercroft was discovered here in 1900 and excavated in 1985–6 following the demolition of the site. The cellar, along with the bridge foundations, is now in the basement of John Lewis's awaiting redisplay to the public.

The Guildhall, 1937. This was built on the site of Clattern House, which in the nineteenth century had been used along with the town hall for local government. More space was needed so the Guildhall was built in 1935.

Queen Elizabeth II leaving the Guildhall, 24 March 1961. The Queen had visited Kingston to celebrate the 400th anniversary of the founding of Kingston Grammar School by Queen Elizabeth I.

Alderman W.E. St Lawrence Finny being awarded the freedom of the borough, 1946. Dr Finny had been mayor of Kingston seven times and did much to instill a sense of pride in Kingston's townsfolk.

Alderman Frederick Gould as mayor, 1880. He was partly responsible for the laying out of both Queens Promenade and Canbury Gardens although he was against the preservation of the Fairfield. He is best remembered for preserving the right of way along Warren Road against the wishes of the Duke of Cambridge.

Councillor H.C. Cooper, Mayor of Richmond, Councillor C.L. Sinclair, Mayor of Kingston and Councillor J.W. Nicholls, Mayor of Twickenham prepare to celebrate the Three Towns Pageant of 1951.

Surrey County Hall, 1896. Surrey County Council was formed in 1889 and, after some debate, decided to have its headquarters in Kingston. County Hall was built in 1893 by C.H. Howell, the County Surveyor.

The Grove in Penrhyn Road, 1897. This substantial house was the residence of the novelist Rhoda Broughton in the 1860s and '70s. It was demolished to make way for a Kingston Polytechnic extension.

The junction of Penrhyn Road and St James's Road, 1905. On the right is The Watersplash, a ford across the Hogsmill river which was not bridged here until 1938. The site was transformed in 1987 by the construction of College Roundabout.

Hog's Mill (known at this time as New Mill) by Denmark Road, 1907. On the site of one of Kingston's Domesday mills of 1087, this mill closed in 1891 and was demolished in 1936.

Clattern Bridge over the Hogsmill, 1898. The arches are part of the earliest bridge which is first mentioned in 1293. However, it could be as much as a hundred years older.

The other (south-east) side of Clattern Bridge showing Victorian arches from one of the many widenings. This picture was taken in 1935 prior to further widening.

The Old Post House restaurant, High Street, in 1954, shortly before its demolition as an unsafe structure. Despite the date on the front, the building dated from the early sixteenth century and was originally The Crane Inn.

Thomas Abbott's contribution to the coronation pageant of 1902. The tricyclists are called 'Well Mended' and 'Crazy Patchwork' after real china vases that were mended and created by Thomas Abbott, a local china dealer.

The Old Malt House, High Street, 1948. A sixteenth-century survivor from Kingston's large brewing industry, this building remained in use until around 1890. It was 'accidently' demolished in 1965, six weeks after gaining a building preservation order.

Portsmouth Road in flood, November 1894. Harris & Son, the ironmongers, is the building in the background. Earlier floods had swamped the Market Place itself, but dredging has now made the Thames more tame.

The Congregational church in Eden Street, *c.* 1910. Built in 1854–6, this stands on the site of an earlier church dating from 1803, and a seventeenth-century Quaker meeting house. Renovated in 1977, it still flourishes today.

The Three Compasses in Eden Street, 1905. This centuries-old Kingston inn was reputedly frequented by the highwayman Jerry Abershaw. The Three Compasses was pulled down in 1974.

The Hand and Mace, 1831. This building housed the unlikely combination of public house and debtors' prison; the former paying for the upkeep of the latter. This site is now part of Bentalls in Clarence Street.

Clarence Street, 1905. The wooden cottage in the middle was pulled down in 1906 to make space for the trams. The Kings Arms on the right followed suit in the 1920s as Clarence Street became a busy thoroughfare.

Another view of Clarence Street in 1905, this time closer to the bridge, which is in the vicinity of the trees in the background. The street off to the left is Church Street.

Clarence Street looking west from Eden Street, 1954. The site of the Kings Arms is under Hambridge's on the right. The trams have come and gone and trolley buses ply the route.

Clarence Street on a Saturday, 1958, taken from Bentalls looking east. To help solve Kingston's traffic problems Clarence Street was made one-way in 1962.

Clarence Street photographed by Les Kirkin on 26 July 1989, the last day before the congestion was solved by pedestrianizing Clarence Street and opening the new relief road under John Lewis's.

Frank Bentall's original store at No. 31 Clarence Street, 1912. At this time he had just purchased R.W. Evans next door. This gave him the whole frontage from No. 25 to No. 43 apart from No. 33, which was not obtained until the 1920s.

Bentall's store in 1935 at the Clarence Street/Wood Street corner just prior to its demolition and the creation of the famous Hampton Court façade.

An aerial view of 1937 showing Bentalls in all its glory with All Saints Church at bottom right. All the buildings on the left have now disappeared under John Lewis's and the relief road.

The Elite cinema on the corner of Richmond Road and London Road, 1954. Built in 1921, the cinema was demolished in 1955. To the left is the Granada of 1939.

The same junction in 1959 showing C & A, which replaced the Elite, and a pair of trolley buses before they were phased out in 1961.

Cliff Richard photographed by Les Kirkin at the Regal, Richmond Road, March 1962. Although it was a cinema, the Regal often staged live shows until it became a bingo club in 1976.

Vine House in London Road, 1900. This eighteenth-century house was allowed to fall derelict in the 1970s, but was rescued by Haslemere Estates who turned it into offices and restored its original appearance.

A tram at the junction of London Road and Richmond Road, *c.* 1910. This tram is going up Kingston Hill to the George and Dragon where the tracks stopped – they never reached Putney as was originally intended.

Kingston station and the railway bridge over Richmond Road, looking north, *c.* 1910. After its mistake in allowing the Portsmouth railway to go through Surbiton in 1838, Kingston did not have its own railway station until 1863.

Councillor Henry Minnitt, Mayor of Kingston, drives the first Kingston tram on 1 March 1906 in London or Richmond Road. Sir Clifton Robinson, the tramway's general manager, stands on the footplate.

St Luke's Church, Gibbon Road, *c.* 1910. The church was built between 1888 and 1891 to serve the fast-growing population of North Kingston. Lady Wolverton paid £1,000 for the spire to be built to make the church more prominent, as she had been unable to find it on her first visit.

Canbury Gardens featuring the bandstand, 1891. The gardens were laid out in 1890–1, the bandstand being a gift from C.E. Nuthall, a former mayor. It was removed in the 1950s.

A group of Sopwith Aviation employees, 1919. Sopwith had two factories in Kingston during the First World War, one in Canbury Park Road, the other at Richmond Road, Ham. These men are from the woodworking section.

Sopwith Dolphins under construction at Sopwith's Richmond Road factory, December 1918. With the war over, the factory was left with hundreds of planes that nobody wanted.

The Canbury Park Road site in the 1930s when it had become Hawker Aircraft. Hurricanes were manufactured here during the Second World War.

The de-burring shop at Hawkers in Canbury Road, 1943. Only one bomb fell on the factory during the war, scoring a direct hit on the first-aid centre.

The drawing offices at Hawker's Canbury Road site. Tommy Sopwith's original office has been preserved but the rest of the Canbury Road site was demolished in 1995.

The horse fair at Kingston, 24 November 1866. The horse fair used to be held in the area north of the church called Horse Fair, but was moved to the Fairfield in 1866.

The cattle fair, at the Fairfield, November 1907. The Fairfield was enclosed and saved as a public space by three-times mayor John Williams in 1865. Several market functions were then transferred here from the Market Place.

The Kingston Tudor Pageant on the Fairfield, 1917. Staged as part of a war market to raise money, this pageant starred the Marchioness of Townshend as Elizabeth I.

The Jubilee Fair on the Fairfield, 1935. In celebration of King George V's twenty-five years on the throne, this fair continued deep into the night and was rounded off by a huge firework display.

A helicopter landing on the Fairfield, 1955. About to climb out is Eddie Calvert, 'The Man with the Golden Trumpet', arriving to play a concert at the Regal. Probably the first helicopter seen in Kingston, it drew a huge crowd.

Tiffin Boys' School on the Fairfield, 1895. Built in 1880, this school was partly funded by a charitable trust set up by Thomas and John Tiffin in 1638 and 1639.

The opening of Kingston Free Public Library, May 1903. Thomas Lyne is the mayor, and on the other side of the mayoress is Andrew Carnegie who helped pay for and who opened the library.

Unveiling the South African War memorial window at the library, June 1905. Lord Middleton is inspecting the troops. Thirty-four men are listed on the memorial.

'King John's Pillar', February 1899. This architectural feature was excavated near Clattern Bridge and now stands in the grounds of the public library. It dates closer to 1300 than to the time of King John.

The Watersplash in Brook Street, 1906. This ford over the Hogsmill with its separate footbridge was a centuries-old feature of Kingston until it was bridged in 1938.

Oil Mill Bridge at Oil Mill Lane, *c.* 1925. The name comes from the nearby mill which ground down linseed for its oil. The road became Villiers Road in 1921.

A flower painting competition is today's lesson at Bonner Hill School in 1908. Opened in March 1906, the school closed in 1980 and was demolished in 1983.

Section Two

NORBITON

Members of the Bunyan Baptist Sunday School, Norbiton, taking part in the coronation day procession of 1902 in Fife Road.

The Fighting Cocks in London Road, 1898. When this pub was demolished and rebuilt in around 1900, traces of two cock-fighting pits were found in the yard.

The Fighting Cocks as represented in the Tudor pageant for Kingston War Market in 1917.

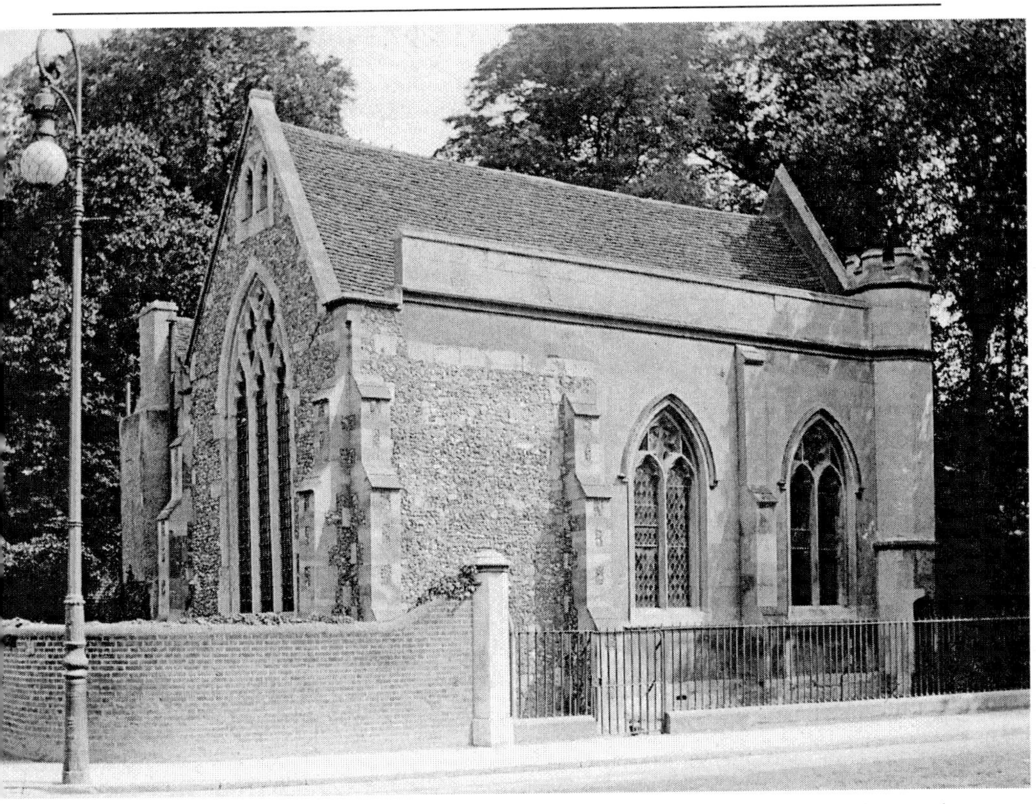

Lovekyn Chapel, London Road, 1897. A chantry chapel called St Mary Magdelene and founded in 1309 by John Lovekyn, this building became Kingston Grammar School in 1561 following its confiscation at the reformation. It has recently been restored as a concert hall and meetings venue, which is a vast improvement on its previous uses as a gymnasium and woodwork classroom.

George V's Silver Jubilee procession in London Road. The float is Bentall's Fairy Queen and her flower fairies.

Another float from the same procession in May 1935. Here are the boys of Kingston Grammar School dressed in Elizabethan costume riding on top of a replica Lovekyn Chapel.

Cleaves Almshouses in London Road, 1897. Founded in 1668 thanks to a bequest from the will of William Cleave, these houses for six poor men and six poor women are still in use today.

St Peter's Church, Norbiton, *c.* 1900. Kingston's population had started to boom in the early nineteenth century and a new church was essential. St Peter's was built in 1842 and thrives today.

St Peter's Day School group photograph, *c.* 1908. Unfortunately, none of the boys' names nor the master's are known.

St Peter's Day School, 1927/8. Another salvaged photograph with little information to support it. This was apparently an outing by the choir.

Harry Webb's butcher's shop in Cambridge Road showing their Christmas turkey display in the 1930s. Harry and Walter Webb stand in the doorway.

Harry Webb's delivery van, 1928.

Kingston Infirmary, 1911. Built in 1897 as an adjunct to the workhouse, the infirmary changed its name to Kingston and District Hospital after the First World War. This building still survives despite some rebuilding and further extensions in recent years.

Royal Cambridge Home for Widows, Cambridge Road, *c.* 1900. Founded in 1852 as a home for widows of NCOs and privates of Her Majesty's Land Forces, this building was destroyed by bombing in 1944 and two widows were killed. The home later moved to East Molesey while this site is covered by flats of the Cambridge Gardens Estate.

Section Three

THE RIVER

A riverside scene, 1906. Kingston regattas occupying the Thames from the bridge to Raven's Ait in the south of Surbiton were a feature of late Victorian and Edwardian Kingston.

The freeing of Kingston Bridge, 1870. The bridge was built in 1828 to replace a decaying wooden structure and tolls were introduced to pay for it. There was great rejoicing when the tolls were lifted.

An aerial view of Kingston Bridge in 1933 with the Market Place at bottom right. Notice also the many barges on the Thames, which was used more for trade and industry than leisure at that time.

The *Jane Mead*, a Thames barge, unloading at Turk's Boathouse in 1895. Turk's still operates and builds boats on the Thames as it has done for over two hundred years.

Queen's Promenade, Surbiton, *c.* 1910. A quiet day on the river with the island of Raven's Ait in the background.

Regatta Day at Raven's Ait, *c.* 1895. Kingston Regatta at this time was a combination of two earlier regattas, one for gentleman amateurs, and the other for tradesmen.

Kingston Grammar School Four, 1911. These boys won two trophies at the Molesey Regatta in this year. The boy on the left is R.C. Sherriff who later wrote *Journey's End*.

The river was for fun as well as for serious sport. Here is another Edwardian photograph showing a variety of skiffs and punts in action.

A free for all after a regatta at Surbiton, *c.* 1910. This is the sort of scene that gave Jerome K. Jerome his inspiration for *Three Men in a Boat*. Behind the pleasure steamer are the houses of Portsmouth Road.

The Thames, *c.* 1900. Raven's Ait is on the left and the tower of All Saints, Kingston, is just visible in the distance. There is even a Venetian-style gondola on the river!

A formation of sailing yachts on the Thames by Kingston Bridge, shortly before the First World War.

St Raphael's Church, 1906. Built as a private chapel by Alexander Raphael in 1846–8, it was the first Roman Catholic church in Kingston since the Reformation.

Section Four

SURBITON

Surbiton Assembly Rooms, c. 1890. Opened in May 1889 after years of effort and false starts, it remains a popular and attractive building despite some thoughtless additions to the façade.

Victoria Road, Surbiton, *c.* 1906, showing the covered trams which were used for the first year of the service. In the background is the junction of St Mark's Hill, St James Road and Claremont Road.

Electric Parade, Brighton Road, *c.* 1905, before the arrival of the trams. The row was named after the building of Surbiton Electricity Works in 1904.

Surbiton Clocktower in Claremont Road, *c.* 1910. Although planned to celebrate Edward VII's coronation in 1902, the clocktower was not completed until 1908 and was never inscribed.

Ewell Road with the council offices on the left and the Methodist church in the distance, 1937. Surbiton war memorial can just be seen in the centre.

Surbiton Council Offices, 1931. Built in 1901–2 for Surbiton Urban District, these became Surbiton Borough Offices in 1936. Since 1966–7 the building has been used as a courthouse.

Clay Lane, 1897. This country lane in Surbiton was named after the local clay used in the nearby brickworks. It was soon built up and named Villiers Avenue in around 1910.

King Charles Road in the 1920s. It was laid out in 1860 and named after Charles I, either in thanks for his charter or in remembrance of a civil war battle in this vicinity in 1648.

The Waggon and Horses, Surbiton Hill, *c.* 1900. This venerable old inn, still owned by Youngs, used to supply extra horses to help pull carts and waggons up Surbiton Hill.

A fire engine in Surbiton, *c.* 1930. The cup displayed on the bonnet is the Challenge Cup awarded to Surbiton Fire Brigade by the Surrey District of the National Fire Engine Association.

Surbiton Cottage Hospital, St James Road, *c.* 1900. Originally opened at York Villa, site of Surbiton post office, the cottage hospital moved to St James Road in 1883.

Surbiton Hockey Club, *c.* 1900. Surbiton is still one of Britain's premier sides and frequently supplies players for the England team.

St Mark's Church, Victoria Road, *c.* 1900. St Mark's was Surbiton's first parish church and was built in 1845. It was largely destroyed by bombing in 1940, but was rebuilt and reconsecrated in 1960.

St Matthew's Church, Ewell Road, *c.* 1900. More churches were needed as Surbiton grew. This one was built in 1874 for £24,000, which was generously donated by Mr Coulthurst.

St Andrew's Church in St Andrew's Road, *c.* 1900. The church was built in 1871–2, and in 1976 the parish was merged with St Mark's.

Kingston Methodist Church, Ewell Road, *c.* 1900. This church was built in 1882.

Christ Church, King Charles Road, 1907. The next church to be built after St Mark's was Christ Church in 1863. However, it needed to be enlarged in 1864, 1866 and 1871, such was the population growth at this time.

Surbiton County School, Surbiton Hill, 1931. This building was originally a private residence, Albury House, which was built in 1856, but was converted to school use in 1926. Now it is part of Hollyfield School.

An aerial view illustrating Surbiton and Tolworth's housing boom in the 1930s. In the foreground is Cranborne Avenue with Largewood Avenue in the centre.

The mayor of Surbiton (Councillor E.B. Ames) signs on volunteers for the Air Training Corps in 1941.

Shere Close, 1952. These council houses, which might be considered to be in Hook, were erected by Surbiton borough following the housing shortage after the Second World War.

Surbiton's third railway station, 1946. The first was little more than a cottage by the track at Ewell Bridge and was built in 1838. The present station was built in 1938, replacing the 1840 station on the same site.

Section Five

TOLWORTH

The opening of Tolworth Fountain, 1903. Built at the junction of Ewell Road and Ditton Road by a generous building contractor, this fountain was demolished in 1936 for road improvements.

Sketches of Tolworth in 1900 before its rapid urbanization. Middle left is a farm by the Ewell Road, and bottom right is a cottage seen from Berrylands path. Bottom left is the pond, which was later filled in and replaced by Tolworth Fountain.

Ditton Road Police Station, *c.* 1910. It was built in 1882 and is still in use today.

Kingston bypass, 1957. Opened in 1927 by the Prime Minister, Stanley Baldwin, this road attracted fast drivers from all over the country.

Hook underpass on Kingston bypass, 1963. The bypass goes down the east side of the borough before rounding Tolworth and passing through Hook. The traffic is no longer so light!

The Tolworth Rise section of Kingston bypass just before the Second World War. Warren Drive is on the left with Beresford and Lyndhurst Avenues in the middle running left to right.

Tolworth Broadway, 1958. This shopping centre, attractive to both cars and pedestrians, is now a busy dual carriageway which can only be crossed at an underpass.

Beresford Avenue, Tolworth, shortly after completion in 1930. Tolworth consists almost entirely of this 1930s housing.

A Royal Windsor Laundry van and driver, 1936. This laundry was founded in Lenelby Road in 1910 by the Groves family and was run by them until the late 1980s.

The Dragonfly branch of the Woodcraft Folk, Tolworth, 1938. Similar to the scouting movement, the Woodcraft Folk was an international group founded in 1925 and is still in operation today.

Boys and girls from eight to eighteen could join the Woodcraft Folk. This display at a fête in around 1938 shows their emphasis on pacifism and cooperation.

Camping and hiking were popular activities of the Woodcraft Folk. This torchlight procession is at a camp in around 1938.

Section Six

HOOK AND CHESSINGTON

Chessington Lane, c. 1910. This is the southern end of Green Lane where it meets Chalky Lane. It is still a picturesque spot today.

A Hook Bowls Club outing, *c.* 1910. The van used for the occasion is Edward Middleton's laundry van, which is parked outside the Southborough Arms.

The choir of St Paul's Church, Hook, seated around Revd Featherstone in 1942. Hook received its own parish as early as 1839, the current church dating from 1883.

Burnt Stub, Chessington, 1938. This mansion was named after stubble burning and not after being burnt down in the Civil War by Cromwell as is often said. It is part of Chessington World of Adventure, formerly Chessington Zoo. Note the elephant loitering by the front door.

Chessington Zoo in the 1950s. This is Pets' Corner showing an early publicity gimmick.

Another view of Chessington Zoo in the 1950s, showing the miniature railway that used to ferry people around. Notice also the Chimpanzee House in the background and a sign to the model railway.

The kennels at Chessington, 1901. Mr Hughes (Whip), Mr A.J. Curnick (Master), Mr Poole (Huntsman), Mr R. Horlick (Hon. Whip), and Mr Lawrence (Second Huntsman) prepare to set out in that once fashionable sport of fox-hunting. Although still fairly rural, there is no longer any fox-hunting in Chessington; the nearest hunt is Surrey Union, based at Cobham.

Harvesting on Park Farm, Chessington, 1906. Chessington is the only really rural part of Kingston borough, but sights like this have of course long gone.

Chessington South station, 28 May 1939, the first day of service. War and the green belt stopped this line continuing to Leatherhead, and the Chessington stations themselves are often threatened with closure.

Section Seven

COOMBE AND KINGSTON HILL

St John the Baptist Church, Robin Hood Lane, Kingston Hill, c. 1905. Built in 1861, this church witnessed the engagement of George V (when he was Prince of Wales) to Mary of Teck.

The George and Dragon, Kingston Hill, on a Sunday morning in 1932. This seventeenth-century inn was redeveloped in 1985 as the Kingston Lodge Hotel.

Two views of Coombe or Tudor Conduit on Kingston Hill, 1937. Along with Gallows and Ivy Conduit, Coombe Conduit supplied spring water to Hampton Court Palace. They were built by Cardinal Wolsey in the early sixteenth century.

The tug of war at the Coombe and Malden Flower Show, 22 July 1908. The two postcards were taken with a wide-angle lens to catch this scene of Coombe men (on the left) defeating Malden men.

Coombe and Malden Flower Show, 22 July 1908. This more sedate scene shows the musical entertainments and the marquees for the flower exhibits in the background.

The club house, Coombe Hill Golf Course, 1938. Opened in 1911, the course was threatened with being sold for housing in 1931, but was rescued by Malden & Coombe Urban District Council in 1934 for posterity.

Section Eight

OLD AND NEW MALDEN

St John the Baptist Church, Old Malden, c. 1900. Called Old to distinguish it from New Malden in the 1870s, Malden dates back to Domesday.

The Bones Gate, Old Malden, 1892. The sign above the door reads: 'This gate hangs well and hinders none, Refresh and pay and travel on.'

The Bones Gate about ten years later with the addition of a new lamp over the side door. The rumour that the name comes from a plague pit is false. It is simply named after a man called Bon or Bone.

Percy Gardens, 1959. These homes for senior citizens are built on the site of an Iron Age, and later Roman, settlement which was partially excavated in the late 1940s and again in 1983.

The railway over Kingston Road, New Malden, 1907. This is the first day of the service from Kingston through to Raynes Park, which accounts for the crowd.

A tram outside the Duke of Wellington public house in Kingston Road, also on the first day of service in 1907.

The Baptist chapel in Kingston Road, New Malden, *c.* 1900. This chapel was built in 1891 replacing an earlier chapel that had stood there since 1875.

New Malden Baptist Chapel after the raid of 16 August 1940. This very heavy bombing raid included a direct hit on the chapel which had to be demolished. A new chapel was opened in 1953.

Fire at a rubber dump in St John's Road, 22 May 1950. It took sixty firemen three hours to get this under control, by which time there was a 500 ft column of smoke visible 20 miles away.

Coombe Road, New Malden, *c.* 1905. The Royal Oak Hotel dates from before 1876 and is still there today.

The club house at Malden Golf Course, 1938. This was built in 1925 when the Raynes Park Golf Club was forced to move to Malden and so changed its name.

New Malden fountain at its opening, 1894. The children on the left are from the New Malden Band of Mercy, which was founded in 1890.

Christ Church, Coombe Road, New Malden, *c.* 1905. Built in 1865 on land given by the Duke of Cambridge, Christ Church was consecrated by the Bishop of Winchester in 1866.

New Malden fountain after May 1914. Here the solitary gas lamp has been replaced by a double lamp following an early traffic accident. The fountain was destroyed by another traffic accident in 1932.

The police station by the fountain in Burlington Road, complete with its staff, *c.* 1910. The police station opened in 1892 and is still in use today.

The first tram to pass through New Malden on its way to Raynes Park, 27 April 1907. This view is from the police station.

A Rifle Club Procession in the High Street, 1907. This is taken from near the railway bridge, with Dukes Avenue on the left just before the bank building. This is now Barclays Bank, but the shops between Duke's Avenue and the railway were demolished in 1963.

Another procession of men in the High Street. This was in 1915 when the rifles were needed. It was a recruiting march for volunteers for the First World War.

The High Street looking north in the 1930s. Sussex Road is on the left just before the Plaza cinema.

J. Sainsbury's 1923 Christmas turkey display at 66 Malden Road (High Street). Sainsburys closed in 1990 and is now the site of Blockbuster video.

New Malden Picture Theatre, May 1922. Opened in 1921, this cinema changed its name to the Plaza in 1929 before burning down in 1936. It is now the site of McDonald's burger restaurant.

New Malden Bridge and railway station, 1959. The bridge is being rebuilt while the road is given a much needed widening.

Council Offices, Malden Road, *c.* 1905, shortly after they were built. The tower is part of the fire station next door.

J.E. Bignall in 1919. He became chairman of Malden & Coombe Urban District Council from 1921 to 1924 and was also a county alderman for Surrey from 1926 until his death in 1930.

Mr Lewis, the first chief of New Malden Fire Brigade, photographed in 1899.

New Malden Fire Brigade showing off its horse-drawn engines for the last time, 1927. Captain Charles Kirk is seated in the middle of the 'engine' on the left.

Captain Charles Kirk (standing) with his new motor fire engine, 1927. He served as chief fire officer for 40 years until 1936.

The firemen of New Malden pose with their engine outside the 1905 fire station, which was still in use in 1961 when this photograph was taken.

St James' Mission Church, Burlington Road, *c.* 1905. This church was built in 1904 but no longer survives. I am not sure when it disappeared.

The College, New Malden, *c.* 1900. Standing opposite the junction of Thetford Road, it was a boarding and day school from before 1884. It became a clothing factory in the First World War for a while, and was finally demolished for the Kingston bypass in the 1920s.

The sorting room in the C.R. Laundry, 1938. The laundry was opened in 1912 by Mr Wild and closed in 1964. C.R. stood for cleanliness and regularity.

A coronation party at the Church Hall in Queen's Road, 2 June 1953. It was probably intended as a street party, but was held indoors because of the dreadful weather that day.

Elm Road, New Malden, *c.* 1905. The housing and the name Elm Road date from the 1860s, but before then this was a track, and was known as Thompson's Lane.

Sandal Dene School for girls, Sandal Road, 1938.

New Malden Drum and Fife Band, 1889. The gentleman on the right at the back with a beard is Mr Davis the band leader.

A family group outside Waslin's hairdressers in Malden Road during or just before the First World War. The old gentleman on the right is Mr Davis the band leader with, it is thought, his adopted son and grandson. Old Mr Davis died in 1918, aged 86.

An unexploded bomb at the corner of The Crescent and Mount Pleasant Road, New Malden, 1941.

Bomb damage in Motspur Park caused by a V-1 which landed between here and Blakes Lane on 3 July 1944. The house on the left is No. 40 Motspur Park. Nos. 42, 44 and 46 have ceased to exist and the clearing up has begun.

Squadron Leader Bazalgette VC. A Canadian living in New Malden at the time of the Second World War, he was killed when his Lancaster was shot down over France in 1944.

Pilot Officer Barton VC from New Malden, who crashed his badly damaged Halifax returning from a raid in 1944, killing himself but saving his crew. Both these VC winners were honoured posthumously, but appear wearing their VC ribbons in these photographs.

Acknowledgements

All the photographs in this book come from the illustrations collection of Kingston Museum & Heritage Service and I am very grateful to them for allowing me to use them in this publication. Kingston has a very full photographic history thanks to the busy picture postcard trade from 1894 and also the founding of Kingston Photographic Society in that same year. Walter Hodgson stands out as one of the best photographers of that generation. More recently I would like to thank Les Kirkin for his pictures from the 1950s to the present day, which keep the collections up to date, and all those people who continue to send in old photographs and postcards. I would like to thank various fellow members of Kingston Museum's staff for their advice and help, and also especially my wife Shaan for encouraging me and allowing me access to her own considerable historical notes on Kingston. I must also thank June Sampson for her many and continuing articles in the *Surrey Comet* as well as for her books listed below.

Bibliography

Margaret Bellars. *Kingston then and now*, Michael Lancet, 1979
Shaan Butters. *The Book of Kingston*, Quotes Ltd, 1995
Stephen Day. *Malden old & new*, Marine Day, 1990
Anne McCormack. *Kingston upon Thames: A pictorial history*, Phillimore, 1989
June Sampson. *The Story of Kingston*, Michael Lancet, 1972
June Sampson. *All change*, News Origin Ltd, 1991
June Sampson. *Kingston & Surbiton old and new*, Marine Day, 1992

BRITAIN IN OLD PHOTOGRAPHS

ALDERNEY

Alderney: A Second Selection, *B Bonnard*

BEDFORDSHIRE

Bedfordshire at Work, *N Lutt*

BERKSHIRE

Maidenhead, *M Hayles & D Hedges*
Around Maidenhead, *M Hayles & B Hedges*
Reading, *P Southerton*
Reading: A Second Selection, *P Southerton*
Sandhurst and Crowthorne, *K Dancy*
Around Slough, *J Hunter & K Hunter*
Around Thatcham, *P Allen*
Around Windsor, *B Hedges*

BUCKINGHAMSHIRE

Buckingham and District, *R Cook*
High Wycombe, *R Goodearl*
Around Stony Stratford, *A Lambert*

CHESHIRE

Cheshire Railways, *M Hitches*
Chester, *S Nichols*

CLWYD

Clwyd Railways, *M Hitches*

CLYDESDALE

Clydesdale, *Lesmahagow Parish Historical Association*

CORNWALL

Cornish Coast, *T Bowden*
Falmouth, *P Gilson*
Lower Fal, *P Gilson*
Around Padstow, *M McCarthy*
Around Penzance, *J Holmes*
Penzance and Newlyn, *J Holmes*
Around Truro, *A Lyne*
Upper Fal, *P Gilson*

CUMBERLAND

Cockermouth and District, *J Bernard Bradbury*
Keswick and the Central Lakes, *J Marsh*
Around Penrith, *F Boyd*
Around Whitehaven, *H Fancy*

DERBYSHIRE

Derby, *D Buxton*
Around Matlock, *D Barton*

DEVON

Colyton and Seaton, *T Gosling*
Dawlish and Teignmouth, *G Gosling*
Devon Aerodromes, *K Saunders*
Exeter, *P Thomas*
Exmouth and Budleigh Salterton, *T Gosling*
From Haldon to Mid-Dartmoor, *T Hall*
Honiton and the Otter Valley, *J Yallop*
Around Kingsbridge, *K Tanner*
Around Seaton and Sidmouth, *T Gosling*
Seaton, Axminster and Lyme Regis, *T Gosling*

DORSET

Around Blandford Forum, *B Cox*
Bournemouth, *M Colman*
Bridport and the Bride Valley, *J Burrell & S Humphries*
Dorchester, *T Gosling*
Around Gillingham, *P Crocker*

DURHAM

Darlington, *G Flynn*
Darlington: A Second Selection, *G Flynn*
Durham People, *M Richardson*
Houghton-le-Spring and Hetton-le-Hole, *K Richardson*
Houghton-le-Spring and Hetton-le-Hole: A Second Selection, *K Richardson*
Sunderland, *S Miller & B Bell*
Teesdale, *D Coggins*
Teesdale: A Second Selection, *P Raine*
Weardale, *J Crosby*
Weardale: A Second Selection, *J Crosby*

DYFED

Aberystwyth and North Ceredigion, *Dyfed Cultural Services Dept*
Haverfordwest, *Dyfed Cultural Services Dept*
Upper Tywi Valley, *Dyfed Cultural Services Dept*

ESSEX

Around Grays, *B Evans*

GLOUCESTERSHIRE

Along the Avon from Stratford to Tewkesbury, *J Jeremiah*
Cheltenham: A Second Selection, *R Whiting*
Cheltenham at War, *P Gill*
Cirencester, *J Welsford*
Around Cirencester, *E Cuss & P Griffiths*
Forest, The, *D Mullin*
Gloucester, *J Voyce*
Around Gloucester, *A Sutton*
Gloucester: From the Walwin Collection, *J Voyce*
North Cotswolds, *D Viner*
Severn Vale, *A Sutton*
Stonehouse to Painswick, *A Sutton*
Stroud and the Five Valleys, *S Gardiner & L Padin*
Stroud and the Five Valleys: A Second Selection, *S Gardiner & L Padin*
Stroud's Golden Valley, *S Gardiner & L Padin*
Stroudwater and Thames & Severn Canals, *E Cuss & S Gardiner*
Stroudwater and Thames & Severn Canals: A Second Selection, *E Cuss & S Gardiner*
Tewkesbury and the Vale of Gloucester, *C Hilton*
Thornbury to Berkeley, *J Hudson*
Uley, Dursley and Cam, *A Sutton*
Wotton-under-Edge to Chipping Sodbury, *A Sutton*

GWYNEDD

Anglesey, *M Hitches*
Gwynedd Railways, *M Hitches*
Around Llandudno, *M Hitches*
Vale of Conwy, *M Hitches*

HAMPSHIRE

Gosport, *J Sadden*
Portsmouth, *P Rogers & D Francis*

HEREFORDSHIRE

Herefordshire, *A Sandford*

HERTFORDSHIRE

Barnet, *I Norrie*
Hitchin, *A Fleck*
St Albans, *S Mullins*
Stevenage, *M Appleton*

ISLE OF MAN

The Tourist Trophy, *B Snelling*

ISLE OF WIGHT

Newport, *D Parr*
Around Ryde, *D Parr*

JERSEY

Jersey: A Third Selection, *R Lemprière*

KENT

Bexley, *M Scott*
Broadstairs and St Peter's, *J Whyman*
Bromley, Keston and Hayes, *M Scott*
Canterbury: A Second Selection, *D Butler*
Chatham and Gillingham, *P MacDougall*
Chatham Dockyard, *P MacDougall*
Deal, *J Broady*
Early Broadstairs and St Peter's, *B Wootton*
East Kent at War, *D Collyer*
Eltham, *J Kennett*
Folkestone: A Second Selection, *A Taylor & E Rooney*
Goudhurst to Tenterden, *A Guilmant*
Gravesend, *R Hiscock*
Around Gravesham, *R Hiscock & D Grierson*
Herne Bay, *J Hawkins*
Lympne Airport, *D Collyer*
Maidstone, *I Hales*
Margate, *R Clements*
RAF Hawkinge, *R Humphreys*
RAF Manston, *RAF Manston History Club*
RAF Manston: A Second Selection, *RAF Manston History Club*
Ramsgate and Thanet Life, *D Perkins*
Romney Marsh, *E Carpenter*
Sandwich, *C Wanostrocht*
Around Tonbridge, *C Bell*
Tunbridge Wells, *M Rowlands & I Beavis*
Tunbridge Wells: A Second Selection, *M Rowlands & I Beavis*
Around Whitstable, *C Court*
Wingham, Adisham and Littlebourne, *M Crane*

LANCASHIRE

Around Barrow-in-Furness, *J Garbutt & J Marsh*
Blackpool, *C Rothwell*
Bury, *J Hudson*
Chorley and District, *J Smith*
Fleetwood, *C Rothwell*
Heywood, *J Hudson*
Around Kirkham, *C Rothwell*
Lancashire North of the Sands, *J Garbutt & J Marsh*
Around Lancaster, *S Ashworth*
Lytham St Anne's, *C Rothwell*
North Fylde, *C Rothwell*
Radcliffe, *J Hudson*
Rossendale, *B Moore & N Dunnachie*

LEICESTERSHIRE

Around Ashby-de-la-Zouch, *K Hillier*
Charnwood Forest, *I Keil, W Humphrey & D Wix*
Leicester, *D Burton*
Leicester: A Second Selection, *D Burton*
Melton Mowbray, *T Hickman*
Around Melton Mowbray, *T Hickman*
River Soar, *D Wix, P Shacklock & I Keil*
Rutland, *T Clough*
Vale of Belvoir, *T Hickman*
Around the Welland Valley, *S Mastoris*

LINCOLNSHIRE

Grimsby, *J Tierney*
Around Grimsby, *J Tierney*
Grimsby Docks, *J Tierney*
Lincoln, *D Cuppleditch*

Scunthorpe, *D Taylor*
Skegness, *W Kime*
Around Skegness, *W Kime*

LONDON

Balham and Tooting, *P Loobey*
Crystal Palace, Penge & Anerley, *M Scott*
Greenwich and Woolwich, *K Clark*
Hackney: A Second Selection, *D Mander*
Lewisham and Deptford, *J Coulter*
Lewisham and Deptford: A Second Selection, *J Coulter*
Streatham, *P Loobey*
Around Whetstone and North Finchley, *J Heathfield*
Woolwich, *B Evans*

MONMOUTHSHIRE

Chepstow and the River Wye, *A Rainsbury*
Monmouth and the River Wye, *Monmouth Museum*

NORFOLK

Great Yarmouth, *M Teun*
Norwich, *M Colman*
Wymondham and Attleborough, *P Yaxley*

NORTHAMPTONSHIRE

Around Stony Stratford, *A Lambert*

NOTTINGHAMSHIRE

Arnold and Bestwood, *M Spick*
Arnold and Bestwood: A Second Selection, *M Spick*
Changing Face of Nottingham, *G Oldfield*
Mansfield, *Old Mansfield Society*
Around Newark, *T Warner*
Nottingham: 1944–1974, *D Whitworth*
Sherwood Forest, *D Ottewell*
Victorian Nottingham, *M Payne*

OXFORDSHIRE

Around Abingdon, *P Horn*
Banburyshire, *M Barnett & S Gosling*
Burford, *A Jewell*
Around Didcot and the Hagbournes, *B Lingham*
Garsington, *M Gunther*
Around Henley-on-Thames, *S Ellis*
Oxford: The University, *J Rhodes*
Thame to Watlington, *N Hood*
Around Wallingford, *D Beasley*
Witney, *T Worley*
Around Witney, *C Mitchell*
Witney District, *T Worley*
Around Woodstock, *J Bond*

POWYS

Brecon, *Brecknock Museum*
Welshpool, *E Bredsdorff*

SHROPSHIRE

Shrewsbury, *D Trumper*
Whitchurch to Market Drayton, *M Morris*

SOMERSET

Bath, *J Hudson*
Bridgwater and the River Parrett, *R Fitzhugh*
Bristol, *D Moorcroft & N Campbell-Sharp*
Changing Face of Keynsham, *B Lowe & M Whitehead*
Chard and Ilminster, *G Gosling & F Huddy*
Crewkerne and the Ham Stone Villages, *G Gosling & F Huddy*
Around Keynsham and Saltford, *B Lowe & T Brown*
Midsomer Norton and Radstock, *C Howell*
Somerton, Ilchester and Langport, *G Gosling & F Huddy*
Taunton, *N Chipchase*
Around Taunton, *N Chipchase*
Wells, *C Howell*
Weston-Super-Mare, *S Poole*
Around Weston-Super-Mare, *S Poole*
West Somerset Villages, *K Houghton & L Thomas*

STAFFORDSHIRE

Aldridge, *J Farrow*
Bilston, *E Rees*
Black Country Transport: Aviation, *A Brew*
Around Burton upon Trent, *G Sowerby & R Farman*
Bushbury, *A Chatwin, M Mills & E Rees*
Around Cannock, *M Mills & S Belcher*
Around Leek, *R Poole*
Lichfield, *H Clayton & K Simmons*
Around Pattingham and Wombourne, *M Griffiths, P Leigh & M Mills*
Around Rugeley, *T Randall & J Anslow*
Smethwick, *J Maddison*
Stafford, *J Anslow & T Randall*
Around Stafford, *J Anslow & T Randall*
Stoke-on-Trent, *I Lawley*
Around Tamworth, *R Sulima*
Around Tettenhall and Codsall, *M Mills*
Tipton, Wednesbury and Darlaston, *R Pearson*
Walsall, *D Gilbert & M Lewis*
Wednesbury, *I Bott*
West Bromwich, *R Pearson*

SUFFOLK

Ipswich: A Second Selection, *D Kindred*
Around Ipswich, *D Kindred*
Around Mildenhall, *C Dring*
Southwold to Aldeburgh, *H Phelps*
Around Woodbridge, *H Phelps*

SURREY

Cheam and Belmont, *P Berry*
Croydon, *S Bligh*
Dorking and District, *K Harding*
Around Dorking, *A Jackson*
Around Epsom, *P Berry*
Farnham: A Second Selection, *J Parratt*
Around Haslemere and Hindhead, *T Winter & G Collyer*
Richmond, *Richmond Local History Society*
Sutton, *P Berry*

SUSSEX

Arundel and the Arun Valley, *J Godfrey*
Bishopstone and Seaford, *P Pople & P Berry*
Brighton and Hove, *J Middleton*
Brighton and Hove: A Second Selection, *J Middleton*
Around Crawley, *M Goldsmith*
Hastings, *P Haines*
Hastings: A Second Selection, *P Haines*
Around Haywards Heath, *J Middleton*
Around Heathfield, *A Gillet & B Russell*
Around Heathfield: A Second Selection, *A Gillet & B Russell*
High Weald, *B Harwood*
High Weald: A Second Selection, *B Harwood*
Horsham and District, *T Wales*
Lewes, *J Middleton*
RAF Tangmere, *A Saunders*
Around Rye, *A Dickinson*
Around Worthing, *S White*

WARWICKSHIRE

Along the Avon from Stratford to Tewkesbury, *J Jeremiah*
Bedworth, *J Burton*
Coventry, *D McGrory*
Around Coventry, *D McGrory*
Nuneaton, *S Clews & S Vaughan*
Around Royal Leamington Spa, *J Cameron*
Around Royal Leamington Spa: A Second Selection, *J Cameron*
Around Warwick, *R Booth*

WESTMORLAND

Eden Valley, *J Marsh*
Kendal, *M & P Duff*
South Westmorland Villages, *J Marsh*
Westmorland Lakes, *J Marsh*

WILTSHIRE

Around Amesbury, *P Daniels*
Chippenham and Lacock, *A Wilson & M Wilson*
Around Corsham and Box, *A Wilson & M Wilson*
Around Devizes, *D Buxton*
Around Highworth, *G Tanner*
Around Highworth and Faringdon, *G Tanner*
Around Malmesbury, *A Wilson*
Marlborough: A Second Selection, *P Colman*
Around Melksham, *Melksham and District Historical Association*
Nadder Valley, *R. Sawyer*
Salisbury, *P Saunders*
Salisbury: A Second Selection, *P Daniels*
Salisbury: A Third Selection, *P Daniels*
Around Salisbury, *P Daniels*
Swindon: A Third Selection, *The Swindon Society*
Swindon: A Fourth Selection, *The Swindon Society*
Trowbridge, *M Marshman*
Around Wilton, *P Daniels*
Around Wootton Bassett, Cricklade and Purton, *T Sharp*

WORCESTERSHIRE

Evesham to Bredon, *F Archer*
Around Malvern, *K Smith*
Around Pershore, *M Dowty*
Redditch and the Needle District, *R Saunders*
Redditch: A Second Selection, *R Saunders*
Around Tenbury Wells, *D Green*
Worcester, *M Dowty*
Around Worcester, *R Jones*
Worcester in a Day, *M Dowty*
Worcestershire at Work, *R Jones*

YORKSHIRE

Huddersfield: A Second Selection, *H Wheeler*
Huddersfield: A Third Selection, *H Wheeler*
Leeds Road and Rail, *R Vickers*
Pontefract, *R van Riel*
Scarborough, *D Coggins*
Scarborough's War Years, *R Percy*
Skipton and the Dales, *Friends of the Craven Museum*
Around Skipton-in-Craven, *Friends of the Craven Museum*
Yorkshire Wolds, *I & M Sumner*